from I N Demmon Kendallville Indiana

THE

PRINCIPLES AND OBJECTS

OF THE

Religious Reformation,

URGED BY A. CAMPBELL AND OTHERS,

BRIEFLY STATED AND EXPLAINED

BY

R. RICHARDSON.

Third Edition, Revised and Enlarged.

CINCINNATI:
PUBLISHED BY H. S. BOSWORTH.

THE PRINCIPLES AND OBJECTS OF THE Religious Reformation,

URGED BY A. CAMPBELL AND OTHERS,

BRIEFLY STATED AND EXPLAINED

BY

R. RICHARDSON.

Third Edition, Revised and Enlarged.

CINCINNATI:
PUBLISHED BY H. S. BOSWORTH.

STEREOTYPED BY L. JOHNSON & CO.
PHILADELPHIA.

CONTENTS.

INTRODUCTORY REMARKS, *page* 5.—The Reformation designed to remove sectarism, ib.—Based on the two great principles of Protestantism, ib.—Seeks to effect union upon a simple evangelical Christianity, 7.—Truths developed in its progress, ib.

I. DISTINCTION BETWEEN FAITH AND OPINION, *page* 8.—Not recognised by sectarism, ib.—Human theories blended with Scripture truths, ib.—Authority of Revelation thus impaired, 9.—Scriptures mean what they say, 10.—True religious faith, ib.—Opinions have no authority, ib.—Agreement in opinion not required, 12.—Objections answered, 14.—Errorists, 16.—Scriptures their own expositor, 17.—How to be studied, ib.—Difficulties in the Bible, 18.—Knowledge progressive, 19.—Textuary preaching, 20.—Protestants debarred from exercising the right of private judgment, ib.—Faith and opinion defined, 22.—Sectarian vocabulary, 23.—Names of sects, ib.—Names adopted in Reformation, 24.

II. THE CHRISTIAN FAITH, *page* 25.—Orthodoxy, ib.—Distinction between the Christian faith and knowledge, ib.—The Christian faith not *doctrinal, but personal*, 26.—Confession of Christ, ib.—Contrasted with theological systems, 27.—Common Christianity, 28.—Import of word *Christ*, ib.—Of the proprosition that *Jesus is the Christ*, 30.—Nature of the Christian faith, ib.—Is trust in a person, 31.—Object of the Evangelists, 32.—The gospel, 34.—Means of salvation, 35.—Means of triumph, 36.—The Christian creed, 37.

III. BASIS OF CHRISTIAN UNION, *page* 39.—*The Christian faith* the only true basis, ib.—Sufficiently comprehensive, 40.—Does not involve controversy, 42.—The capital fact of revelation, 43.—A Divine oracle, 45.—The rock on which the church is founded, 46.—The good confession for which Christ died, 47.—Confession of first converts, 48.—Objections answered, 50.—Divinity of Christ, 51.—Change of heart, 52.—True repentance, ib. —Reconciliation, 54.—Detection of heresy, 55.

IV. REMEDIAL INSTITUTIONS, *page* 55.—Often blended, 56.—Patriarchal institutions, 57.—The Mosaic system, ib.—Christianity, 58.

V. COMMENCEMENT OF THE CHURCH, *page* 59.—Mistakes respecting it, ib.—Day of Pentecost, ib.—Church began at Jerusalem and not at Rome, 61.—Impartation of the Holy Spirit, 62.

VI. ACTION AND DESIGN OF BAPTISM, *page* 63.—Reformers pedobaptists, ib.—Questions concerning baptism, ib.—Design of baptism, 68.—Its emblematic character, 71.—Sects *transfer* the office of baptism to emotions, 72.

VII. AGENCY OF THE HOLY SPIRIT, *page* 74.—Source of error, ib.—Conversion and sanctification different, ib.—Reception of the Spirit, 75.—Given to the children of God, ib.—Regeneration, 76.—Gift of the Holy Spirit the great end of the gospel, 78.—To be sought by prayer, 79.—Fruits of the Spirit, ib.—Obstacles to conversion, 80.—Controversy here uncalled for, ib.—All things of God, 82.

VIII. WEEKLY COMMUNION, *page* 83.—A practice of primitive church, ib.—Its neglect regretted by the learned and pious, 84.—Testimony of Brown of Haddington, ib.—Of the Archbishop of Dublin, ib.—Of Dr. Scott, ib.—Of Dr. Mason, ib.—Of Calvin, 85.—Of Wesley, ib.

IX. CHURCH GOVERNMENT, *page* 85.—Pastors, elders or bishops, ib.—Why known by different titles, 86.—Their qualifications and duties, ib. —A plurality in each church, ib.—No bishop over a diocese, ib.—Popes and prelates, ib.—Apostolic succession, ib.—Deacons, 87.—Evangelists, ib.—Conclusion, ib.

PRINCIPLES AND OBJECTS

OF THE

REFORMATION.

Bethany, Va., September, 1852.

MY DEAR F.:—I proceed, according to promise, to lay before you the general principles and objects of the Reformation which has been, for some time, urged upon the religious communities, both of this country and the British Isles. And this I do with the more pleasure, as I know you have not given heed to those misrepresentations by which its enemies have endeavored to impede its progress, and that you are, yourself, sensible of the many evils induced by that sectarism from which it is the great purpose of the present Reformation to relieve society.

Let me observe, then, in the first place, that this religious movement is wholly based upon the two great fundamental principles of Protestantism, viz.:

1. The Bible is the only Book of God.
2. Private judgment is the right and duty of man.

All Protestants assert the truths of these propositions, and cling to them as the theory of the original Reformers, who protested against the authority claimed by priests and popes to dictate articles of belief. But it is unhappily true, that the party dissensions of Protestants have insensibly led them to depart, in practice, from both these cardinal principles. In direct opposition to a most obvious deduction from the *first*, they have exalted human systems of theology to an authority equal, if not paramount, to that of the Bible. At the same time, in violation of the *second* of these principles, they deny to the people the privilege of interpreting the Bible otherwise than in accordance with these systems. A human standard of orthodoxy is thus, in fact, substituted for the Bible; and, by a natural and inevitable consequence, the Bible has become a sealed book to the masses, who do not, because they dare not, understand it for themselves.

Such being, in few words, the actual state of the religious community, the present Reformation proposes an immediate return to the broad and original platform of Christianity, as well as of true Protestantism; and urges, accordingly, the claims of the Bible alone, as the source of Divine truth for all mankind; and pleads for the exercise of man's inalienable right to read and interpret the Sacred Volume. It seeks to establish a *unity of faith*, instead of that *diversity of opinion* which has distracted religious society; and to restore the gospel and its institutions, in all their original simplicity, to the world. In brief, its great purpose is *to establish* CHRISTIAN UNION *upon the basis of a* SIMPLE EVANGELICAL CHRISTIANITY.

Having thus given you a general statement of the purpose of this religious movement—a purpose which cannot fail to be approved by the truly pious of all parties—I now proceed to lay before you the important distinctions and truths which have been developed during its progress. And in this place I would remark, that, as the character of prevailing errors always determines, in advance, the issues which are to be made by the advocates of truth, so, certain fundamental points of great importance have been thus forced upon the attention of the friends of the Reformation, as matters requiring, in the very first instance, to be elucidated and determined. Among these I would mention—1st. The distinction between FAITH and OPINION. 2d. The distinction between what may be emphatically termed THE CHRISTIAN FAITH and doctrinal KNOWLEDGE. 3d. The true BASIS OF CHRISTIAN UNION. Amongst the important subjects which have been brought into view during the progress of the Reformation, I would invite your attention, in continuation, to the following: —4th. The distinction between the Patriarchal, the Jewish, and the Christian dispensations. 5th. The commencement of the Christian church. 6th. The action and the design of baptism. 7th. The agency of the Holy Spirit in conversion and sanctification. 8th. Weekly communion; and 9th. Church government. Upon each of the above topics, I desire now to give you, as briefly as possible, the views of the Reformers.

I. Distinction between Faith and Opinion.

This distinction is of the utmost importance, and lies at the very threshold of religious reformation and Christian union. Without a proper recognition of the difference between FAITH and OPINION it is impossible to make any progress in a just knowledge of Divine things, or to obtain any clew by which the mind can be extricated from the perplexed labyrinth of sectarism. Notwithstanding, however, that it is so important to distinguish between these things which are so radically different from each other, they are everywhere confounded; the fallible deductions of human reason are continually mistaken for the unerring dictates of inspiration, and human authority is blended with that which is Divine. Human opinions, indeed, are the plastic cement in which partyism has imbedded the more solid yet disconnected scriptural materials of its partition walls. Or, to employ another figure, a theory, consisting of any number of favorite opinions, smoothly intertwined, forms the thread upon which various Scripture doctrines and texts are strung and curiously interwoven, so as to assume a form and meaning wholly artificial and unauthorized.

When men thus fail to make any distinction between the express *revelations* of God and the *opinions* which men have superadded, and when they have already committed the great error of adopting indiscriminately, in the religious system of a party, an incongruous mixture of opinions with the things of faith, the mistiness and obscurity which surround the former overspread by degrees the latter also. Hence it has come to pass that matters of belief and mere speculations upon religious subjects are usually classed together as "religious opinions;" and when we speak of a man's religious opinions, we are constantly understood to mean, or, at least, to include, his belief. Hence, too, the Divine communications themselves have lost much of the authority and respect which are justly due to them, by being thus reduced to a level with human opinions, and by the implication that they are so limited in their range of subjects, and so deficient in clearness, as to require additions and explanations from uninspired and fallible men, in order to render them intelligible and complete. The question, accordingly, is no longer, "What *say* the Scriptures?" "How *readest* thou?" "What hath the Lord *spoken?*" but, What do the

Scriptures *mean?* What thinkest *thou?* What do the *standards* of my church or the *leaders* of my party say?

In opposition to views and practices so erroneous, we urge—

1. That the Scriptures mean precisely *what they say*, when construed in conformity with the established laws of language.

2. That the Bible contains the only Divine revelations to which man has access; and that these revelations are perfectly suited, by their Divine Author, to the circumstances and capacity of man to whom they are addressed.

3. That true religious *faith* can be founded upon this DIVINE TESTIMONY *alone.*

4. That *opinions* are mere inferences of human reason from insufficient and uncertain premises, or conjectures in regard to matters not revealed, and that they are not entitled to the slightest *authority* in religion, by whomsoever they may be propounded.

The measure of faith is, then, precisely the amount of Scripture testimony, neither more nor less. What this distinctly reveals, is to be implicitly believed. Where this is obscure or silent, reason must not attempt to elaborate theories or supply conclusions, and impose them upon the conscience as of Divine authority. By the practical recognition of this principle, the theological systems and theories which have distracted religious society, are at once deprived of all their fancied importance, and, consequently, of all their power to injure. Those remote speculations; those metaphysical subtleties; those untaught questions which have occupied the minds of the religious public, to the exclusion of the all-important, yet simple truths of the gospel, are at once dismissed as the futile reveries of uninspired and fallible mortals. When these are thus dismissed, *the human mind is left alone with the word of God.* It is brought into direct contact with the Divine law and testimony, from which alone the light of spiritual truth can emanate, and this light is no longer obscured by the mists of human opinionism and speculation.

If this distinction were duly appreciated by the Protestant world, there would be a speedy end of those controversies by which it has been so long disturbed. For it is undeniable, that there is an almost universal agreement among the various evangelical denominations, in regard to the great revealed truths of Christianity; and that they are separated, alienated and belligerent, for the sake of certain favorite opinions, which have been promulged by their founders. Each one admits that there exists this common Christianity, apart from denominational peculiarities, and that salvation is possible in any of these parties; yet each continues to urge its distinctive tenets, and maintain its peculiar opinions, as though the salvation of the world depended upon these alone. Human opinions and speculations, then, have manifestly too much authority with the religious public, and are too highly honored in being made the great objects for which each party lives and labours. If, then, they were clearly distinguished from the revealed truths, upon which, like parasites, many of them have grown; if they were fairly separated from all connection with the Divine testimony, from which they derive a stolen nourishment and a borrowed vigor, they would appear at once in their true character, as matters wholly foreign and insignificant, and would be allowed to droop and perish with all the bitter fruits they have so profusely borne.

It is preposterous to expect that men will ever agree in their religious opinions. It is neither necessary nor desirable that they should do so. It is no where commanded in the Scriptures that men should be of one opinion. It is there declared that there is "ONE FAITH," but is no where said that there is one opinion. On the contrary, differences of opinion are distinctly recognised, and Christians are expressly commanded to receive one another without regard to them. (Rom. xiv. 1.) As well might we expect to conform the features of the human face to a single standard, as to secure a perfect agreement of men's minds. Hence there can be no peace, unless there be *liberty of opinion.* Each individual must have a perfect right to entertain what opinions he pleases, but he must not attempt to enforce them upon others, or make them a term of communion or religious fellowship. They can do no harm, so long as they are private property, and are regarded in their true light, as human opinions *possessed of no Divine authority or infallibility.* It is quite otherwise, however, when leading and ambitious spirits take them for the warp and the Scriptures for the woof from which they weave the web of partyism. The flimsy and ill-assorted fabric may please the taste of the few, while it will be despised and derided by those who manufacture an article no better from similar incongruous materials, and thus a contention is perpetuated, with which human selfishness and pride have much more concern than either piety or humanity.

It is, accordingly, one of the primary objects of the present Reformation to put an end to all such controversies, by reducing human opinions to their proper level, and elevating the word of God, as the only true standard of religious faith. Hence it was, in the very beginning, resolved to "reduce to practice the simple original form of Christianity, expressly exhibited upon the sacred page, without attempting to inculcate any thing of human authority, of private opinion, or inventions of men, as having any place in the constitution, faith, or worship of the Christian church; or any thing as matter of Christian faith or duty, for which there cannot be expressly produced a Thus saith the Lord, either in express terms or by approved precedent."*

Every proposition or doctrine, then, for which there is not clear scriptural evidence, is to be regarded as a matter of opinion; and every thing for which such evidence can be adduced, is a matter of faith—a fact or truth to be believed. It may be objected here, that what may be clear to one mind may be doubtful to another; and that the Scriptures are constantly appealed to, by all parties, as affording to each sufficient proof of its peculiar views, which, in each case, conflict more or less with those of every other party. This may be true, but what follows? That the Scriptures are themselves a tissue of contradictions and ambiguities? That it is impossible to determine their true meaning? Nay, truly, this were to deny the fundamental principles of Protestantism, viz. the Divine origin of the Bible, and the right of private interpretation. For God could not be the author of a volume of this character; and the right to interpret the Scriptures, presupposes the ability to

* Declaration and Address of the Christian Association of Washington, p. 4.

comprehend them, since, without this, to concede the right would be but mockery.

The facts involved in the above objection may be readily accounted for, without impugning either the Divine origin or the intelligibility of the Bible. They are such as must necessarily occur when men adopt false rules of interpretation,* or come to the Scriptures with minds already biassed in favor of particular views. The intelligibility of the Bible is not *absolute*, but *relative*, depending as much upon

---

* Among the most prolific sources of error in religion is the practice of taking isolated texts of Scripture, and giving to them a meaning and application never intended by the writers. Of this nature is the fallacy employed by the Westminster and other confessions, in the numerous Scripture references appended to each article of the creed. These are taken as proofs by those who are too indifferent or too indolent to ascertain, by an actual examination of the context, that the passages so referred to have, in most cases, little or nothing to do with the particular matter to which they are applied. There are not wanting many, however, who, even with the passages before them, would regard the least *allusion* to the subject as abundant proof of any proposition which might be offered in regard to it. Hence the easy credulity of those who believe the doctrines of the textuary preacher.

To obtain the true sense of Scripture we must carefully inquire—1st. *What* is said? 2d. *Who* says it? 3d. To whom or of whom is it spoken? 4th. Under what *circumstances* was it said?—and we must always take the language in its proper connection with what precedes and what follows.

the state of mind of him who reads it, and the method he pursues, as upon the perspicuity of the book itself. All Protestants assert that the way of salvation is clearly defined in the Sacred Volume, so as to be plain to the most ordinary comprehension. If, then, erroneous views be formed from it, the cause is to be sought, not in the Bible, but in the mind of the errorist himself. He comes to the Scriptures as an *advocate* of preconceived opinions or doctrines, to seek for proofs and arguments by which to sustain these views; and not, as a sincere inquirer after truth, to engage in a process of careful *investigation*, and with a mind prepared to follow whithersoever the truth shall lead. Hence it is, that all errorists and parties holding sentiments the most discordant, have recourse alike to the Bible for their proofs. They seek not for the truth which is in the Bible, but for proofs of the errors with which their minds are previously imbued—for something to sustain the particular system to which they are inclined. To them the Bible is a mere storehouse of arms and ammunition for partisan warfare. It has no well-defined plan or purpose of its own, but is merely a collection of proof-texts, from which any one is at liberty to select whatever may appear to suit his purpose, without respect to the context, or the laws of interpretation applied to all other writings. Thus it is that the Bible answers the purposes of all parties equally well. As with the mirror of the Arabian tale, each one can see in it only what he wishes to see; and as each party wishes to see only itself, the Divine mirror reflects to its view no other image. A man would not be more surprised to see, in the glass before which he stands, the image of his enemy, instead of his own, than would be the advocate of one party to find in the Bible the views of an opposite sect. It must be evident, that to treat the Bible thus, is grossly to abuse the most precious gift of Heaven, and to sustain, by a mere pretence of Divine authority, a system of partyism and contention wholly incompatible with the express purpose of Christianity, and the conversion and salvation of the world. He who would understand the Divine communications must study them with the humility and docility of a child; he must prayerfully endeavor to ascertain the meaning of the *text* by the *context*, making the Scriptures *their own expositor*, and must give himself up to be led by them, instead of presuming to lead them to his own favorite and preconceived opinions, by wresting and perverting them from their true meaning and application.

He, then, who will thus devote himself to the study of the Bible, will not long remain either in ignorance, error, or doubt, as to the great matters of faith and duty. It is distinctly affirmed in the Book itself, that "the Inspired Scriptures are profitable for all things; for doctrine, for reproof, for correction and instruction in righteousness, that the man of God may be perfect, and thoroughly furnished unto every good work." If, then, the believer may be thus perfected, thus thoroughly furnished, what needs be more? Most assuredly, if the Book of God appear in any case to fail thus to enlighten the mind and direct the conduct, we may in vain expect that any volume from fallible and uninspired men could supply the deficiency and secure these objects.

To acknowledge that there are certain difficulties in regard to *some* matters of Holy Writ is but to concede the depth and vastness of its themes, and the deficiency of fallen man in his powers of comprehension, and in his aptitude to receive spiritual truths. Unquestionably, there are some subjects too mysterious in their nature to be clearly explained in human language; some too great to be completely grasped by a finite mind; many too remote from the ordinary range of human thought, to be distinctly apprehended by the most discerning intellect. As, in the natural heavens we have bodies so remote that they appear but as faint nebulæ, and stars which can scarcely be distinguished by human vision from those which cluster around them, so have we, in the Book of God, glimmerings of spiritual systems far distant from our own, whose relations to us we may never comprehend in our present state of being.

Such must necessarily be the case in regard to communications concerning the Divine Creator and the things of an infinite, unseen, spiritual world. These are subjects to be reverently pondered and contemplated only so far as, upon the heavenly scroll, we may discover their outline, or discern their more salient points. These are not things about which men may dogmatize; into which they may vainly and presumptuously intrude; or in regard to which they may insolently excommunicate and anathematize each other. To admit, further, that the Bible will not be *at once* equally clear to all minds, even in regard to matters actually developed in it, is only to confess that men are *unequal* in capacity, in spiritual mindedness, and in devotion to the means of biblical knowledge. We may say of the whole Bible, as Peter said of Paul's Epistles, that it contains "some things *hard* to be understood;" which, nevertheless, may be understood through diligent study and proper use of the means of biblical interpretation. Scriptural knowledge is, therefore, progressive, and will vary in different cases, and in the same person, at different periods. There will be always babes, young men, and fathers, in scriptural learning; and hence, there is opportunity to comply with the apostolic injunction—that the elder should teach the younger, and that Christians should edify each other. Hence, too, the use of pastors and teachers, who, in the exercise of their functions, promote the growth and edification of the church.

How different, however, from this primitive state of the Christian church; this mutuality of spiritual edification and growth; this common yet individual interest in the Divine communications, is that imbecile condition of perpetual and hopeless pupilage in which congregations wait for the weekly explication of some fragment of Scripture called a "text;" no member presuming to edify either himself or his brethren by his own researches, or venturing to trust himself to the Word of God, or to advance a single step in scriptural knowledge, lest he should ignorantly miss the path prescribed by church authority, and become entangled in the snares of error! The truth is, that the great mass of Protestants are just as effectually debarred, by clerical influence, from the exercise of the right of private judgment in matters of religion, as are the Romanists themselves by priestly prohibition. They have no confidence in the intelligibility of the Bible, or in any views which they may take from it. An individual, having *once in his life* exercised the right of private judgment, not in regard to the things taught in Scripture, but in choosing between the systems and tenets of different parties, and having adopted the particular system which he prefers, will for ever after rest content with the orthodoxy of his opinions, and give himself little concern about what may be contained in the Scriptures of Truth. One who unites with the church of Rome, must thus far, at least, exercise the right of private judgment in choosing between conflicting claims, and can show subsequently scarcely more indifference to the Holy Volume of inspiration.

Indeed, it were difficult to conceive why, on his own principles, the sectary should make a proper use of the Bible. He may, indeed, read it as a pastime or as a task; he may even feel a certain interest in its historical details, or be more or less impressed with its sublime imagery and powerful diction; but for truly religious purposes it can avail him nothing. Confident that his favorite creed-makers have secured the treasure for his use, he cares but little for the casket, which he thinks himself unable to unlock. Believing them to have traversed the whole area of revelation; to have settled authoritatively all its difficult questions; guarded all its essential truths, and unfolded in a few brief, sententious articles of faith, all its deep and hidden mysteries, what inducement can he have to prosecute research, or bring his mind into direct communication with the Word of God?

In this Reformation, however, it is a fundamental principle that every one shall take his religion directly from the Bible, without the intervention of popes or priests, councils or assemblies, or any of the creeds which they have framed. With us, every thing in religion must have a Scripture warrant, and human authority is regarded as wholly incompetent to the decision of any question which may legitimately arise in regard to the great matters of faith and duty. Whatever rests upon a *Divine warrant* is a matter of FAITH. Whatever subordinate and collateral questions may exist which have not this warrant are MATTERS OF OPINION, which each one is at liberty to entertain according to his own pleasure, and to which no one, from the very nature of the case, can attach any importance. Nor is it to be imagined that any doctrine or sentiment can be justly entertained under the title of an opinion which will conflict with or nullify any portion of Scripture. Where the Bible speaks, there is no place for any opinion; and if any one hold a view which contravenes any declaration of Holy Writ, this is not an opinion, but actual DISBELIEF of so much of the Word of God as is thus contradicted and opposed.

In entire harmony with these views, it is regarded as of the utmost practical importance to speak always of religious matters in the exact language of the Bible. All those unscriptural terms and expressions, of which the modern sectarian vocabulary almost wholly consists, are, accordingly, discarded as conveying ideas more or less foreign from the Bible, and as being in no case so accurate and appropriate as the language of Scripture. It is true, that Bible terms themselves may be misunderstood or misapplied, if the context be not carefully examined; and especially, if a religious theory or favorite practice be in question. But when an individual is *unable* to express his religious sentiments, without using unscriptural expressions, it is *prima facie* evidence that his religious views are not in the Bible. For if they were, he could certainly state them in the exact language of the Sacred Volume. Such is the reciprocal influence of words and thoughts, that any change in the language employed by the inspired writers is to be regarded with suspicion; nor can we suppose it possible to have a restoration of the simple original gospel of Christ and the primitive institutions of Christianity, that is to say, of primitive modes of thought and action, without a return to the primitive modes of expression also. The names, and many of the institutions of the different sects, as well as their modes of speech, are alike utterly unknown to the Bible. As for those who take part in the present Reformation, they desire to have nothing to do with any thing in religion that is not at least as old as the books of the New Testament; and in aiming to restore and obey the simple primitive gospel and its institutions, and to give to these Bible things their Bible names, they desire, also, to assume themselves no other titles than those originally given to the followers of Jesus, viz. DISCIPLES OF CHRIST; CHRISTIANS; THE CHURCH OF CHRIST; or THE CHURCH OF GOD, &c.; all of which are regarded as scriptural, and to be used interchangeably, according to circumstances.

I hope I have been sufficiently explicit upon the distinction to be made between faith and opinion. But now, as faith springs from the Divine testimony, and will be co-extensive, so to speak, with the knowledge which any one may have of that testimony, the question arises, How great must be the extent of this faith, in order to entitle an individual to be received to church membership? In other words, How much of the Bible must he have explored and comprehended, before he makes a profession of Christianity? Must he have examined the whole Divine testimony, in regard to all the subjects of which it treats; or are there particular points or doctrines, to which his attention may be restricted, and in regard to which alone his faith may be properly inquired into and tested? Or, to shorten the question, what is that which is emphatically called "the faith," "the truth"—the belief which "sanctifies" and "saves" the soul? Our views of this I shall now proceed to give you.

II. The Christian Faith.

A thorough knowledge of the Bible is not regarded by any of the sects as an essential prerequisite to a profession of faith. All agree that there are certain fundamental points which must be believed, and which, taken together, constitute what is termed orthodoxy.* To extract these from the Bible has been the great business of councils and assemblies, which, smelting, as it were, in their party furnaces, the ore of Holy Writ, have obtained, as they imagined, from it, the pure and precious metal. This they have then mixed with the requisite portion of alloy to give it *hardness;* and having stamped it with their own theological image and superscription, have issued it as the only standard coin in the realm. Each party, however, disagreeing as to the characters which should distinguish this precious metal, have, unfortunately, obtained a different product, and we have, consequently, in circulation, as many standards as there are parties; and it would puzzle the most skilful assayer in the theological mint to determine their relative values.

Nevertheless, after all, we certainly concur with the rest of the religious world, in making a distinc-

* "Orthodoxy," as Warburton wittily observed, "is *my* doxy, and heterodoxy is *another man's* doxy."

tion between what is properly and especially "the faith," or the Christian faith, and a general belief and reception of the Divine testimony, contained in the canonical books of the Old and New Testaments. But we differ from all the parties here in one important particular, to which I wish to call your special attention. It is this: that while they suppose this Christian faith to be *doctrinal,* we regard it as *personal.* In other words, they suppose doctrines, or religious tenets, to be the subject-matter of this faith; we, on the contrary, conceive it to terminate on a *person*—THE LORD JESUS CHRIST HIMSELF. While they, accordingly, require an elaborate confession from each convert—a confession mainly of a doctrinal and intellectual character, studiously elaborated into an extended formula—we demand only a simple *confession of Christ*—a heartfelt acknowledgment that *Jesus is the Messiah, the Son of God.*

The Christian faith, then, in our view, consists not in any theory or system of doctrine, but in a sincere belief in the person and mission of our Lord Jesus Christ. It is personal in its subject, as well as in its object; in regard to him who believes, as well as in regard to that which is believed. It consists of simple facts, directly connected with the personal history and character of Jesus Christ as the Messiah and the promised Lamb of God who takes away the sins of the world. It is personal in its object, leading to personal regard and love for Christ, and a personal interest in his salvation. It consists not in definitions; neither does it embrace the litigated questions of sectarism. It contains not one, much less five cardinal points of speculative theology; nor does it inflict upon the believer, for his sins, *forty articles save one.* The gospel of salvation, indeed, were ill-fitted to be preached to every creature, illiterate or learned, if it consisted, as some imagine, of those ponderous bodies of divinity, and intricate systems of theology, which have oppressed the energies and entangled the movements of the Protestant world.

It has been, indeed, the great error of Protestants, and the great cause of all their schisms, that they have sought to supersede this direct personal reliance upon Christ, by a mere intellectual assent to a set or system of tenets. True, they do by no means proscribe this personal trust or faith in Christ, but the natural working of the whole machinery of a party, so far as it is peculiar and denominational, tends to lead the mind away from this simple faith to a false confidence in mere human opinions and intellectual abstractions, and in outward forms. Thanks, however, to the power of the gospel itself, this tendency of the systems of the day has been checked in individual cases; and, though many are lulled into a false security, trusting to the orthodoxy of their belief, and mistaking a zeal for human opinions as a meritorious earnestness for saving truth; and substituting an extravagant admiration of the leading men and favorite preachers of their denomination for the love of Christ, there are some who have gazed, in silence and in secret, upon that face "marred;" that form insulted; those bleeding wounds of that Just and Holy One who "offered himself without spot to God," and have, in humble hope, yielded to him alone their confidence and love. Such individuals are found in all parties, and they recognise each other as being fellow-heirs of the grace of life, and as having a common interest in the great Redeemer. It is, indeed, this simple faith in Christ, accompanied by its appropriate fruits, which constitutes that "common Christianity" which is admitted to exist in all parties, independent of party peculiarities; an admission, by the way, which at once assigns to these peculiarities their true character, as mere excrescences upon Christianity; as having no power to save, and as the very means of perpetuating division. Happy would it be for the world, if all could be induced to rest content with that "common Christianity," which it is the very object of the present Reformation to present to the religious community as the only means of securing unity and peace.

I am aware, that it will be difficult for those who

have been accustomed to regard the Christian faith as an assent to a particular set of tenets, to recognise this simple belief in Christ as sufficient to admit an individual to the blessings of Christianity. If, however, they will fully consider the scriptural import of this faith in Christ, they will perceive, that, under an extreme simplicity which adapts it to all minds, it necessarily involves and includes all the conditions of salvation. It is to be noted, that to believe in Christ is not simply to believe what Christ says; that is, to receive as true whatever may be regarded as the teaching or doctrine of Christ. This is the very inadequate and erroneous view which we have been combating, which mistakes an intellectual assent to the deductions of reason from Scripture premises, or even to the express dictates of inspiration, for a personal and direct reliance upon Christ himself. Again: to believe in Christ is not merely to believe that there lived a person bearing that name. Yet there are multitudes who seem to have no higher idea of the Christian faith than this, and no better knowledge of the term Christ than to suppose it a mere personal appellation. But the word Christ is not a name. It is an official designation. The *name* Jesus, given by express command of God, is itself significant, and the addition of the word CHRIST, with the definite article, which is often expressed and may be always supplied, furnishes the titular and qualifying expression which denotes the peculiar character of the person. He is not *Jesus Christ*, as an individual thus named and surnamed, but he is JESUS THE CHRIST. These are propositions totally different. The former might be to us of no peculiar moment; but the latter expands itself over the past, the present, and the future, and involves in it the eternal destinies of the human race. Yet, though to believe the person to whom this title is applied to be what the title really imports, is to believe something concerning this person, of a most important and far-reaching nature, even this would fall short of constituting the Christian faith, if this conviction be supposed unconnected with that *trust* and *direct reliance* upon this person which would be justly due to him in the office and character thus assigned to him.

Whether or not it be possible for any one fully to understand the import and bearings of the sublime proposition that *Jesus of Nazareth is the Christ*, and truly to believe it, and yet, at the same time, to entertain the proposition as a mere intellectual conviction, without giving up the heart to him in humility, penitence, and love; to trust and confide in him as the only Saviour, and the anointed King of kings, is a question which I deem it unnecessary here to consider. For certain it is, that if it be possible for any one thus to separate, in point of fact, words from thoughts, thoughts from things, or things from the emotions they are fitted to excite, and to believe this proposition as a mere doctrine, tenet, or mental abstraction, such a one does not possess the Christian faith. To believe in Christ, is to receive him in all the glory of his character, personal and official; to trust in him in all the relations which he sustains to us, as our Prophet, our Priest, and our King; to behold in him our only hope and refuge; and renouncing ourselves, our own self-confidence, our righteousness, and every vain device, to lean on him only as our stay, and to look to him only as the "Lord our Righteousness," as our salvation and our life. It is not merely to believe what is said of him as the Son of God; as the Son of Man; as living, dying, rising, reigning, returning; but, believing this, to trust in him as *our* Saviour, to walk with him as *our* teacher, *our* friend; to realize his gracious presence with us, and to discern his footsteps in the path we tread. It is to be brought into *direct relation* and *fellowship* with him; to think of him as of a *person* whom we know, and to whom we are known; to speak to him as to one who hears, and to listen to him as to one who speaks. Such, in our view, is the Christian faith; not a trust in definitions; in doctrines; in church order; in apostolic succession or official grace; in opinions or dogmas, true or false; but a sincere belief of the testimony concerning the facts in the personal history of the Lord Messiah, accompanied by a cordial reception of him in his true character as thus revealed to us, and an entire *personal* reliance upon him for our salvation.

That this simple trust in Jesus, and nothing else, is really and truly "the faith," will be clearly seen by any one who will examine the Scriptures upon the subject. He will there find:

1st. That the history of Jesus of Nazareth is related to us—his birth, his miracles, his teachings, his sufferings, his glorification; and that our attention is called to the fulfilment of the ancient prophecies, in the incidents recorded of him, for the express purpose of producing this faith. I need only here refer to the close of the testimony of John, where he expressly declares this to have been the object: "And many other signs truly did Jesus in the presence of his disciples, which are not written in this book; but these are written that ye might believe that Jesus is the Christ, the Son of God."*

* Nothing contributes more to a correct view of Scripture than a knowledge of the particular *design* of each of its main divisions. John, as here quoted, expressly states the immediate purpose of his "gospel" or testimony to be to produce the belief that Jesus is the Christ, the Son of God. That Matthew, Mark, and Luke had the same object in view is perfectly apparent from the nature of the facts they relate and the application they

2d. That Jesus himself declares, that "God so loved the world that he gave his only begotten Son, that *whosoever believeth in him should not perish, but have eternal life.*" And he announces, also, on the other hand, that it is the rejection of this faith which occasions condemnation. "*He that believeth not* is condemned already, because *he has not believed on the name of the only begotten Son of God.*" And many other passages might be quoted of the same purport.

---

make of them. The four "gospels" are *concurrent* testimonies, and their concurrence is additional evidence of the truth of the facts recorded; which facts are selected and arranged with special reference to their force and fitness as *proofs* of the great proposition above mentioned. Again, in the "Acts of the Apostles," we have a special purpose, viz. to show how the apostles fulfilled the commission they had received from Christ, in opening the kingdom of heaven—1st. To the Jews, as related in the 2d chapter; 2d. To the Samaritans, as reported in the 8th chapter; and 3d. To the Gentiles, as recorded in the 10th chapter: the call of the latter being still further exhibited in Paul's travels and labors. Many other matters also of great importance are stated, as the descent of the Holy Spirit, the proceedings of the primitive churches, &c. So, also, with regard to the Epistles; each one has its particular purpose. The letter to the Romans develops, in a continuous argument, the great doctrine of "justification by faith," in opposition to the Jewish view of the efficacy of the works prescribed by the Mosaic law. The letter to the Hebrews presents also a continuous argument to show the superiority of Christ to Moses; of the Christian institution to the Jewish, &c. A clear view of the design of each epistle is thus a key to its interpretation.

3d. That he commissioned the apostles "to go out into all the world and preach the gospel to every creature," declaring that he that believed and was baptized should be "saved," and that he that believed not should be "condemned." Now, "the gospel" is simply the glad tidings concerning Christ; that "he died for our sins according to the Scriptures, was buried and rose again, according to the Scriptures." (1 Cor. xv. 3, 4.) It consists of the simple story of the cross; of those wonderful facts in Christ's history which reveal him as the promised Lamb of God, who should take away the sins of the world. To believe these facts is to receive Jesus as the Christ, the Son of God, and the Saviour of men.

4th. That the apostles, in fulfilling this commission to preach the gospel, gave to those whom they addressed, a concise statement of these facts in Christ's history, and presented the evidence on which they rested; thus endeavouring to produce in the minds of their hearers this belief in Jesus as the Messiah, and requiring no larger faith than this, and no more extended knowledge than this involves, for introduction into the Kingdom of Christ.*

* Take, for example, Peter's discourse, Acts ii.: "Ye men of Israel, hear these words: Jesus of Nazareth, a man approved of God among you by miracles and wonders, and signs which God did by him in the midst of you, as ye yourselves also know; Him, being delivered by the determinate counsel and

5th. That this faith in Christ is that which is expressly enjoined in order to salvation. See the address of Paul and Silas to the Philippian jailer, Acts xvi. 31—"Believe on the Lord Jesus Christ, and thou shalt be saved." Or Philip's declaration

---

foreknowledge of God, ye have taken, and by wicked hands have crucified and slain; whom God hath raised up, having loosed the pains of death, because it was not possible that he should be holden of it. * * Therefore, being by the right hand of God exalted, and having received of the Father the promise of the Holy Spirit, he hath shed forth this, which ye now see and hear. * * Therefore, let all the house of Israel know assuredly that God hath made that same Jesus, whom ye have crucified, both Lord and Christ."

The effect of this discourse was, as we are told, that three thousand persons were pierced to the heart and converted to Christ. Or, take, in the following chapter, Peter's address to a different audience: "The God of Abraham, and of Isaac, and of Jacob, the God of our fathers, hath glorified his Son Jesus; whom ye delivered up, and denied him in the presence of Pilate, when he was determined to let him go. But ye denied the Holy One and the Just, and desired a murderer to be granted unto you, and killed the Prince of Life, whom God hath raised from the dead, whereof we are witnesses." The result of this was, we are told, that about five thousand men "believed." "Howbeit, many of them which heard the word believed; and the number of the men was about five thousand." Or take the first discourse to the Gentiles: "The word which God sent unto the children of Israel, preaching peace by Jesus Christ, (He is Lord of all.) That word, I say, ye know, which was published throughout all Judea and began from Galilee, after the baptism which John preached; how God anointed Jesus of Nazareth with the Holy Ghost, and with power; who went about doing

to the eunuch, Acts viii. 37—"If thou believest, with all thy heart, thou mayest;" and the satisfactory reply, "I believe that Jesus Christ is the Son of God." Again: John says, "This is his commandment, that we should believe on the name of his Son Jesus Christ, and love one another, as he gave us commandment."

6th. That it is this faith which not only introduces the believer into the Christian institution, but enables him to maintain his profession and sustain himself against the temptations of life. "Whosoever shall confess that Jesus is the Son of God, God dwelleth in him and he in God." Again: "Whosoever is born of God, overcometh the world; and this is the victory that overcometh the world, even our faith. Who is he that overcometh the world, but he that believeth that Jesus is the Son of God?"

---

good and healing all who were oppressed of the devil, for God was with him. And we are witnesses of all things which he did, both in the land of the Jews and at Jerusalem; whom they slew and hanged on a tree. Him God raised up the third day and showed him openly; not to all the people, but unto witnesses chosen before of God, even to us, who did eat and drink with him after he rose from the dead. And he commanded us to preach unto the people, and to testify that it is he which was ordained to be the judge of quick and dead. To him give all the prophets witness, that, through his name, whosoever believeth in him shall receive remission of sins." Or, again, take Paul's preaching at Antioch, Acts xiii. 17–41, &c.

But I need not multiply quotations to show that a sincere belief in Jesus as the Christ, the Son of God, is emphatically and truly *the Christian faith*, and the only faith which can lawfully be demanded in order to admission to Christian privileges and church fellowship. This is the CHRISTIAN'S CREED, and the only creed to which any one may be justly called upon to subscribe. And this being so, all other creeds and confessions are at once nullified and repudiated, as without Divine authority, and mere inventions of men, leading the mind away from Christ, and from a direct and personal reliance upon him, to mere intellectual conceptions, abstract propositions, and human opinions; or, if not wholly to these, at least to subordinate truths, collateral questions, remote conclusions, which belong not immediately to what is properly the Christian faith, but to the subsequent chapter of Christian knowledge. Hence, even upon the hypothesis that the religious formularies of doctrine now in vogue contain nothing but truth, we deny the right of any one to complicate the simplicity of the Christian faith in this manner, and to demand, in advance, a degree of knowledge and experience in the child, which, in the very nature of things, can be expected only in one who has attained to the stature of a man in Christ Jesus.

It will appear, then, from the above, that, while

we regard the whole Bible as the only repository of true knowledge in religion, and as the volume which is to occupy the mind and heart of the Christian student, we consider that particular portion of it which is immediately concerned with Christ's personal history and ministry, as that which is to be presented to the unconverted world as embracing the subject-matter of the Christian faith—the simple gospel of Christ. This may be either read in the book itself, or presented by the living preacher. "Faith comes by hearing, and hearing by the word of God." It is a plain and simple narrative, the truth of which was confirmed by signs and miracles; "those demonstrations of the Spirit" which attended its introduction, and which were then faithfully recorded, in order to accomplish the same purpose in all future ages. It is this gospel which is the "power of God for salvation, to every one who believes it." It is not *a* power of God—*one* of the methods which God employs to save; but it is emphatically *the* power of God for salvation; the only revealed way in which God can, in consistency with his own attributes, justify and save the sinner. It is the cordial belief of this love of God, thus manifested in the life, death, resurrection, and glorification of Christ, which reconciles man to God, which overwhelms the soul in penitence and contrition for its offences, and, through the influences of the Holy Spirit, produces entire renovation of heart and reformation of character. In brief, it is Christ himself who is thus made to us "wisdom" and "righteousness," "sanctification and redemption."

III. The Basis of Christian Union.

Every one will agree, that the true basis of *Christian union* is the CHRISTIAN FAITH. All the parties assert this, but, unfortunately, each one adds to that faith, or, rather, substitutes for it, human opinions, and matters of doctrinal knowledge not immediately connected with salvation; and they refuse to receive each other, because they do not happen to agree in these opinions and doctrines, while, at the same time, they may hold in common what really constitutes the Christian faith. This Christian faith, as we have seen, is simply belief in Christ, as he is presented in the gospel, and it is concisely engrossed in the great proposition that Jesus is the Christ, the Son of God. No one can comprehend the terms of this proposition, without having before his mind the whole Christian faith in its subject matter. The predicate, "the Christ the Son of God," if understood, implies a knowledge of God and a belief in him, and presents to view not only the official character of the Messiah as the *Christed* or *anointed* Prophet, Priest, and King of whom the prophets spoke, but also his personal character or divinity as the Son of God. The subject, "Jesus," is an expression which can be comprehended only as it involves an acquaintance with the personal history of Jesus of Nazareth, and, consequently, of the great facts which constitute the gospel. The whole proposition thus presents to us —Jesus as the Son of God—the Christ, or anointed One, whom God has appointed to be our Teacher, our Redeemer, and our King; to whose precepts we are to listen; through whose precious blood and intercession we are to obtain forgiveness; by whose word and Spirit we are to be sanctified, and by whose mighty power we are to be rescued from the captivity of the grave. As, in nature, the lofty spreading oak was originally contained in the acorn, or, rather, in a single cell of that acorn, upon which were impressed all the nature and laws of development which distinguish the mighty monarch of the woods, so it has pleased God to wrap up, as it were, in a single proposition, that vast remedial system, which may overspread and shelter, in its full development, the whole assembled family of man. In it is presented the simple word, or gospel, which is most appropriately termed "the good seed of the kingdom," and which, when it grows up and is fully matured, produces fruit unto eternal life. It is the same Infinite Wisdom which has dictated the arrangements both of nature and religion. In both, means apparently the most simple, produce the grandest results. In both, the processes are slow and gradual. It is "first the blade, then the ear; then the full corn in the ear." Nowhere is the ground uptorn with sudden violence that the full-grown oak may be planted, or that it may receive into its bosom the spreading roots of grain ready for the sickle. "The Kingdom of God," says the great Teacher, "is as if a man should cast seed into the ground, and should sleep and rise night and day, and the seed should spring and grow up he knoweth not how." It is the simple gospel which is sown in the heart, and not, as sectarians imagine, complete and elaborate systems of theology. *It is with this proposition and its proofs, that God first meets the sinner*, and it is in its cordial reception that the latter finds the grace and mercy of God. Oh! that the sectarian world could thus contemplate this beautiful simplicity of the truth, as originally presented by Christ and his apostles, and, adopting it as the true ground of Christian union, could be induced to forsake for it those confused and complicated systems which have no power either to save sinners or to unite saints.

The above observations address themselves to those who may, at first view, suppose this basis of union to be too narrow, and to contain too little, while, in truth, it contains all, and is the very germ from which the whole Christian institution proceeds. But there are cavillers who may object, on the other hand, that it contains, or rather implies, too much; involving questions about which men will differ. They will say, that there are not only in the above proposition itself, but in the preliminary knowledge which it supposes, many matters about which men may and do disagree; and that this formula, then, however simple and concise it may appear, may, nevertheless, give rise to debate and division. To this I would reply, that we might as readily look for the giving of a law by which men could be justified, as expect to obtain any basis of union, which men, in their pride of opinion and love of controversy, may not make a ground of disunion. It is true, that men have started a great many questions respecting the nature and attributes of God; about the character and sonship of Christ; the method, object, and extent of the atonement, &c. &c.; and that some of the warmest religious disputes are upon these very topics. But these are either untaught questions, with which we have nothing to do, (for we have no business with any religious questions which are not mooted in the Bible,) or they are vain speculations upon matters utterly beyond the reach of the human intellect, or, lastly, they are sublime truths, which can be fully unfolded only in the chapters of Christian knowledge and experience, and in regard to which we have no right to demand, in advance, even that amount of knowledge which the Scriptures themselves furnish when fully explored. All these disputes, in short, are about doctrines, intellectual conceptions, abstract truths; but, as we have endeavored to show, the Christian faith has respect to *facts*, by which we do not mean truths delivered, but things really and actually performed and attested by witnesses. There are, indeed, some general truths, which we must suppose the mind to have received, before it could possibly apprehend the gospel facts. For instance, it must have admitted the being of God. But all such fundamental and elementary truth here required, is either self-evident, or of such a nature that it cannot be supposed absent from the mind. Hence the Bible nowhere attempts to prove the existence of God. It begins by declaring the fact that "God created the heavens and the earth," but it takes for granted the elementary truth that there is a God. Now, the great proposition on which the Christian Institution rests, affirms, in like manner, a simple matter of fact, involving the same elementary truth, which requires no new proof, and can justly give rise to no controversy. It is either the fact that Jesus is the Son of God, or it is not. Upon this question rests the whole Christian fabric, and it is one which is not to be proved by reasoning from abstract principles, but by the testimony of God himself and the evidence of such other facts as are pertinent to the case. Such, accordingly, are the very proofs which are supplied in regard to this great basis of Christianity, which, like the sun in the heavens, is placed far above all those controversies which have so beclouded the religious parties as almost wholly to conceal its splendor and intercept its life-giving beams. It is in this great fact that the Lord Jesus Christ himself is presented to us in his true and proper character, that we may so receive him and trust in him. He is, indeed, the Sun of Righteousness, the radiating and attracting centre of the spiritual system, shedding light on the heavens and on the earth —upon the things of God, and the nature, duty, and destiny of man. In accepting the above proposition, then, we take Christ himself as the basis of Christian union, as he is also the chief corner-stone and only foundation of the church. To demand, instead of this, as a profession of faith and basis of union, an exact knowledge of remote points of Christian doctrine, is as unscriptural as it would be irrational to prohibit men from enjoying the light and warmth of the natural sun until they had first attained a high proficiency in astronomy, and were able to determine the movements and magnitudes of the remote planets and inferior satellites of the solar system.

Neither do we, on the other hand, at all concede

that this great fact may be confounded with any thing else in the Divine testimony, or that its splendor may be at all diminished by comparison with any one or all other facts presented to the mind. It stands alone in all its sublime grandeur, amid the revelations of God. There is nothing, indeed, which may be justly compared with it. All other propositions in Christianity are subordinate to this, and can be rendered visible only by the light which it sheds upon them. Allow me here to offer a few additional considerations from the Scriptures, which will serve to give a just view of the position which this fact occupies in the Christian institution.

1. The proposition which asserts it is a DIVINE ORACLE, in a specific and peculiar sense, for *it was announced by the Father himself from heaven.* It is seldom, indeed, that God has directly addressed himself to men, and when He lays aside the ordinary methods of communication and presents himself, as it were, in person, to speak to mortals, we may be sure the communication is one of the most transcendent importance. Such was the case when, at the baptism of Jesus, in presence of the assembled multitude upon the banks of the Jordan, there came a voice from heaven, saying, "THIS IS MY BELOVED SON." Such was also the case at the transfiguration, when the same declaration was repeated to the chosen disciples, in presence of Moses the giver, and

Elijah the restorer of the law, with the significant addition, "HEAR YE HIM."

2. *This proposition is the rock upon which Christ himself declared he would build his church.* I refer here to Matt. xvi. 13–19, where we are told that Christ, after inquiring what were the conclusions of the people in regard to him, and receiving, in reply, a statement of their various opinions, put to his own disciples the question, "But who say ye that I am?" To this Peter promptly replied, "Thou art the Christ the Son of the Living God."

This is a most remarkable passage, and is, of itself, quite sufficient to show the position which this declaration occupies. It was because Peter was the first to make this direct confession of Christ, that the Saviour honored him by committing to him the keys of the Kingdom of Heaven; that is, the privilege of opening the gates of this kingdom to the Jews and also to the Gentiles—an office which he fulfilled, as recorded in Acts, chap. ii. and x. This, of itself, indicates the high value attached to this declaration. But we are not left to judge of its importance merely from the honor awarded to him who was the first to make it. Christ himself expressly declares here, referring to Peter's confession of his Divine sonship, that *upon this rock he would build his church,* and that against it, thus founded, the gates of death should not prevail. Now, it must be evident to every mind, that *the foundation of the church can be the only basis of Christian union.* The church is but the general assembly of saints, and the basis on which it rests must, of necessity, be the ground of union and communion of its members. And whatever is a sufficient basis for the whole church, must, of course, be sufficient for each individual member of that church. Upon that basis they can be united together as a church of Christ, and upon no other basis. "Upon this rock," says Jesus, "I will build my church." "Other foundation can no man lay," says Paul, "than that which is laid, which is Jesus the Christ," who was announced in his divine and proper character in the above declaration.

3. This is the "good confession" which Christ himself "witnessed" before his judges, and for which he was condemned to be crucified. During his ministry, he had forbidden his disciples to tell any one that he was the Messiah, reserving to himself to make this confession at this awful moment, before the great tribunal of Israel. When all other evidence had failed his enemies, and he was adjured by the High Priest to say if he was the Christ, the Son of God, he replied in the Hebrew style of affirmation, "Thou hast said." "What further need," cried the High Priest, "have we of witnesses; behold we have heard his blasphemy." And they

answered, "He is worthy of death." Can any thing more clearly display the true character of this great proposition, than the fact that Jesus thus honored it by dying for it? He was himself thus laid as the foundation corner-stone of the church of the Living God.

4. But finally, it is abundantly evident from the Scriptures, that it was this very confession which was made by those who, during the ministry of the apostles, were admitted to the institutions of the gospel and the fellowship of the church. I have already referred you to the discourses of the apostles, which have all the same object—to produce the belief, and, of course, the acknowledgment of this great fact. I need only refer again to the detailed case of the Ethiopian eunuch, who, after JESUS was preached to him by Philip, demanded baptism. Philip said, "If thou believest with all thy heart, thou mayest." And he answered, "I believe that Jesus Christ is the Son of God." We see, then, that as Christ declared he would build his church upon this rock, and was himself laid as its foundation-stone, so the apostles and evangelists proceeded to build upon this tried foundation, as living stones, those individuals who, through this simple faith in Christ, were made alive to God.

From what I have already said, you will doubtless fully comprehend our views of what constitutes the true basis of Christian union. A truth-loving mind is not disposed to cavil, and knows how to select the most favorable point of view from which to judge correctly of the questions at issue.

Sectarians, however, are a race of cavillers. Partyism narrows the mind and perverts its powers, so that it becomes incapable of appreciating or even perceiving the beauty or excellence of truth. Self-satisfied and confident in its own infallibility, it has no love of progress, and desires no change, so that it necessarily opposes itself to any overture that can be made to heal the scandalous divisions that exist, and restore the original unity of the church. It will, doubtless, start many groundless objections to the above basis of union, which are unworthy of notice. There are some, however, sometimes presented, which, as they involve misrepresentations of our views, I will here briefly consider. Thus, it will sometimes be asked, Do you propose, then, to receive persons into the Christian Church upon a simple confession of their belief in Christ as the Messiah, the Son of God, without repentance or change of heart, or even baptism? Would you receive any one to communion with the church upon such a declaration, without any inquiries as to the sense which he attaches to the expression "Son of God," or in respect to his feelings and experience of the grace of God in his heart? May you not thus receive and fraternize with those who are Unitarian or Sabellian in faith, or mere formalists in practice?

As a general answer to all such objections, I might say, that it is enough to know that any course of procedure has a Divine warrant, in order to adopt it without the slightest fear of any consequences which may ensue. But to be more particular, I would say in regard to the reception of those who would attach a peculiar, or Unitarian sense to the words of the above proposition, that such a perversion is a natural result of preconceived theories and speculations, which lead men to explain away the plainest statements of Scripture, or wrest them by specious glosses; and that, since, according to the fundamental principles of this Reformation, all such speculations are to be abandoned, and the word of God itself is to be taken as the guide into all truth, there is not the slightest room for apprehension. And this is, thus far, fully confirmed by our experience; for I presume there is not a religious body in Christendom, which renders a more true and just honor to the Lord Jesus Christ, or receives with a more sincere faith, all that the Scriptures declare concerning him. With us, he is the Son of God, in the strict sense of these words. He is the Word which was in the beginning, which was with God and was God: the Word by whom all things were made; in whom was life, and who became flesh and dwelt among men, revealing his glory—the glory as of the only begotten of the Father, full of grace and truth. He is the brightness of the Father's glory, and the express image of his person. In him dwelleth all the fullness of the Godhead bodily. He is Immanuel, God with us, who, having brought in an everlasting righteousness, and made an end of sin by the sacrifice of himself; and having for us triumphed over death and the grave, has been invested with all authority in heaven and in earth, and has taken his seat at the right hand of the Majesty in the heavens, where he must reign until all his enemies are subdued, and from whence he shall come the second time, in his glory, with all the holy angels, to judge the world. In short, whatever character, office or relation, is assigned to the Father, to the Son, or to the Holy Spirit, in the Sacred Scriptures, we most sincerely acknowledge in the full sense and meaning of the terms employed; and it is for the express purpose of securing the truth, the whole truth, and nothing but the truth, upon this most momentous subject, as well as upon all others in religion, that we desire to adhere to the exact language of the Bible, and repudiate all that scholastic jargon which theologians have presumed to substitute for the diction of the Holy Spirit, and which mystifies, perverts, dilutes, and enfeebles the sublime revelations of God.

With regard to the other inquiry, respecting repentance and a change of heart, we do certainly expect every one who presents himself for admission into the church, to exhibit satisfactory evidences of both. By the word *repentance* we here imply much more than a mere sorrow for sin, which may often exist without producing any amendment of heart or life. Judas is thus said to have "repented;" and persons are often, in this sense, sorry for their actions, because they feel or fear the consequences which flow from them, or because of some transient and superficial impression, and not because they have realized the true nature of sin, the purity and perfection of the Divine character, and their own unworthiness.

In the Greek of the New Testament, two different words, *metamelomai* and *metanoeo,* or the noun *metanoia,* are used to express these two different conditions; but, in the common version, these words are, unfortunately, always rendered "to repent," or "repentance," so that the distinction which is made in the original, does not appear in the translation. Both these words occur in 2 Cor. vii. 10, which reads:—"For godly sorrow works repentance to salvation not to be repented of." We have here what appears to be a play upon words, as Dr. George Campbell observes, which was far from the design of the apostle, who in the first part of the sentence uses the word *metanoia,* but at the close employs the *other* expression. The former denotes not only a sorrow for sin, but such a conviction of its true nature as leads to amendment of life. The latter signifies merely that regret or uneasiness of mind which may exist without any change of conduct. The first involves both repentance, in this limited sense, and what we embrace in the word reformation; so that we approach, perhaps as closely as our language will admit, to the sense of the apostle, by rendering the passage thus: "For godly sorrow works a *reformation* unto salvation, not to be repented of." It is this most comprehensive expression which is employed by Peter, in Acts ii. 38, when, in addressing those who believed his annunciation of Jesus as the Messiah, and were pierced to the heart, he commanded them to "reform." And it is this sincere penitence, accompanied by change of conduct, the proper fruit of reformation, which in our view constitutes the only true evangelical repentance. We do not, however, imagine, as many seem to do, that the sinner can, by this repentance, establish any *claim* upon the Divine mercy; neither do we suppose that by any sort of penance he may acquire *merit* in the sight of Heaven, or perform works of supererogation to be placed to the account of others. And we are just as far from believing that God is yet to be reconciled to the sinner, or that the prayers and tears and penitence which either the sinner, or others in his behalf, may offer, can possibly render God more propitious, or more willing to save. We do not take such a view of the gospel as to perceive any room whatever to call upon God to be reconciled to *men*. On the contrary, we regard the reconciliation as fully accomplished on the part of God through the death of his Son, and that it is MEN who are now required to return to *God*, who is "in Christ reconciling the world unto himself." Hence says Paul, 2 Cor. v. 20: "We are ambassadors for Christ: as though God did beseech you by us, we pray you in Christ's stead, be ye reconciled to God." There is not, indeed, a more unscriptural or anti-evangelical conception, than that the sinner can do any thing, either to atone for his own sins, or induce the Deity, by an act of special or extraordinary grace, to interpose in his behalf, and to renew his heart independent of the gospel. We have no fellowship with any theory which makes the word of God of no effect, or represents God as requiring to be moved with greater love for man than that which he has manifested in the gift of his Son; and we are accustomed to place far more reliance upon a willingness to hear and to obey the Lord's commandments, as an evidence of a change of heart, than upon all those dreams, visions, and animal excitements, on which many are taught to depend for the proof of their conversion. The heart is changed when we love God. It is a Divine philosophy, that, "We love God because he first loved us." And "by this we know that we love God, if we keep his commandments." A sincere belief of the gospel will produce its appropriate fruits, and it is by these alone that we can scripturally recognise the sincerity of the faith and the repentance. Individuals may confess Christ in word, but in works they may deny him. They may call him Lord, but refuse or neglect to obey his commands. And when such persons unite themselves to the church, we find, in their case, the Scriptures no less profitable for *reproof* and *correction*, than they are, in that of the true believer, for "instruction in righteousness."

IV. Patriarchal, Jewish, and Christian Institutions.

Having dwelt so long upon the leading principles of the Reformation, it will now suffice to present a very brief statement of the results proceeding from the practical application of these principles. Among the earliest of them was the discovery that *Christianity is a distinct and peculiar institution, complete in all its parts, and requiring no addition from any system of religion previously established.*

No clear and just distinctions had heretofore been made between the different religions presented in the

Bible; but, on the contrary, such were the confused notions of the religious public, that Christianity was supposed to be merely an emendation of Judaism, as the latter was, in turn, regarded as an improvement upon the more simple system of the patriarchal age. In short, it was supposed that the Bible contained but *one religion;* and it was usual to attempt to cover the confusion of thought and the practical incompatibilities arising from this view, under the notion that this religion was presented in three dispensations, each of which was a modification of the one that preceded it; and that in the form called Christianity, we were to find, as it were, a mere change of external rites, or a substitution of one thing for another, without any radical or essential difference in principle, administration, or authority.

Hence, in different parties, we have so much of Judaism incorporated with Christianity, from the external pomp of Temple-worship and the simulated robes of the Aaronic priesthood, to the more serious commixture of the discordant introductory principles —mere fleshly descent, and a living faith in Christ.

It is not be denied, indeed, that the great principles of religion and morality have been the same in all ages, and that the essential means of access to God and of acceptance with Him, have remained unchanged since the faith of Abel. But it is equally true, that for special purposes, connected with the development of the Divine character and government, there have been established, at different periods of the world's history, peculiar institutions, administrations, or economies, which, differing as they do in most important particulars, it is essential to distinguish from each other, in order to a just comprehension of any one of them. We recognise, then, as remedial systems—1st. The PATRIARCHAL INSTITUTION, which continued from the fall of Adam to the Divine mission of Moses. 2d. The JEWISH RELIGION, which remained in force from Moses until the coronation of Jesus as Lord and Messiah; and 3d. The CHRISTIAN ECONOMY, which continues from that time to the present, and is never to be superseded by any other.

The Patriarchal institutions of religion were adapted to the early period of the world. The head of the family was its officiating priest; religious knowledge rested upon tradition, with special revelations to those who were distinguished for their faith and piety. This age had, accordingly, its own proportion of Divine truth; its own special promises; its peculiar faith; and its appropriate religious rites.

The Mosaic system, also, had its own specific purposes to subserve. It was a theocracy; a peculiar form of government; a civil polity, as it contained the *political* regulations of an entire nation: yet it was, at the same time, a *religion*,* embodying in its precepts, and shadowing forth in the various types and symbols of its elaborate ritual, the most sacred truths, and revealing the Divine character in new and most important lights. As an institution, indeed, it was so peculiar and so different from any other that has ever existed, that there is not the slightest difficulty in determining its nature and defining its boundaries.

Especially is it to be distinguished from Christianity, in whose spiritual and literal truths its carnal and typical observances found their destined fulfilment; and to whose simple faith and all-embracing amplitude, its outward ceremonial and restricted boundaries gave place. Differing thus in its very nature and in its principles of membership, the Jewish institution contrasts with Christianity in all essential points. In its covenants, its promises, its mediator, its priesthood, its laws, its ordinances, and its sanctions, it is exhibited upon the sacred page as wholly diverse from the gospel institution. How indispensable it is, then, to a just view of Christianity, that these important differences, which are so distinctly noted by the apostle to the Gentiles, in

* Paul, in addressing the Galatains (i. 13, 14) says: "Ye have heard of my conversation in time past in the Jews' religion." In Paul's view, then, Judaism was a distinct religion from Christianity.

his Epistles to the Hebrews and Galatians, should be fully understood and acknowledged; and that the simple gospel of Christ should be freed from the corrupting admixture of Judaism, with which it is still contaminated in the minds of so many of the religious public!

V. Commencement of the Christian Church.

The same obscurity which has rested upon the landmarks of the various Divine institutions of which we have spoken, has naturally enveloped, also, the origin of the Christian Church. Some suppose its foundation to have been laid in eternity; others, concluding to await the creation of man, make Adam its first member; others postpone it to the days of Abraham; and not a few make it coeval with Moses. To any one, however, who will trust the Scriptures upon the subject, nothing can be plainer than that the Christian Church commenced its formal existence on the day of Pentecost which immediately succeeded Christ's ascension into heaven. I need here only notice some of the scriptures from which this is abundantly evident.

In the first place, in order to show that it did not originate before Christ's personal ministry, it will be sufficient to quote the express language of Christ himself, who, in reference to Peter's acknowledgment that he was the Messiah, says: "On this rock I will build my church." He here uses the future tense—"*I will build.*" So that the church was not yet founded upon this rock, its only true foundation. Christ himself, indeed, became the chief corner-stone of this spiritual edifice, which is said to rest also upon his apostles and prophets, who were the earliest members and supports of the church.

There are, indeed, some passages which seem to imply that the church had already an existence during the ministry of Christ on earth. These must, however, in harmony with others which are more definite, and with the facts of the case, be understood as spoken prospectively; of which style we have various examples, as, for instance, in the institution of the Lord's Supper, in which Christ speaks of his blood as shed, before the event actually occurred. It is true that the *body*, so to speak, of the church, was prepared during Christ's ministry; and this body was, on the day of Pentecost, quickened by the impartation of the Holy Spirit, just as God first formed the body of Adam, and afterward "breathed into his nostrils the breath of life." Just so, also, in the types of the Jewish religion, the tabernacle and the temple were first prepared, and then the Shekinah or Divine Presence took up his abode in them as the necessary sanction, without which all their religious ministrations would have been unacceptable and invalid. It was not until every thing was finished, and the ark of the Lord placed beneath the cherubims, that fire descended from heaven to consume the offered sacrifice, and that the glory of the Lord filled the temple.* Without the presence of the Holy Spirit, the Church of Christ could have no life, nor power to exercise its functions, nor could it be recognised as distinctly and formally established in the world. Hence the disciples were commanded to "tarry at *Jerusalem*" until they should be "*endued with power from on high,*"† and they were then to proceed to preach the gospel among all nations, "*beginning at Jerusalem.*" This was in accordance with the prophecies of Isaiah and of Micah, that "out of Zion should go forth the law, and the word of the Lord from Jerusalem."‡ So that we have thus distinctively fixed both the *place* and the *time* at which the Christian institution should commence. It was then and there only that all things were prepared. Christ had there offered himself as a sacrifice for the sins of the world, and had thence ascended into the true holy place, to appear in the presence of God, where, having been exalted and crowned "a Prince and a Saviour, to grant repentance and remission of sins," and having,

* 2 Chron. v. 7–13; viii. 1. † Luke xxiv. 49; Acts i. 4.
‡ Isaiah ii. 63; Micah iv. 2.

also, received of the Father the promised Holy Spirit, he communicated, upon that eventful day, those gifts and life-giving energies to his waiting disciples, by which the church was quickened into being, and enabled to assume, for the first time, its distinct and appropriate character and functions. Hence thousands were on this day converted, as related in the second chapter of Acts; and it is in the close of this same chapter that we, *for the first time*, find the church distinctly spoken of as an existing institution. "The Lord," we are told, "added daily to *the church* such as were saved."

We find, then, that the three things required in order to the establishment of the Christian Church were all present upon the day of Pentecost referred to, and at no antecedent period. A body of disciples was then prepared. The Lord Messiah having humbled himself to the death of the cross, was then exalted, and glorified, and constituted head over all things to his church, "which is his body, the fulness of him who filleth all in all." And, lastly, this glorious head then imparted to this body that Holy Spirit which he himself received of the Father, in order that his church might be thus fitted to discharge its appropriate functions, and that its members might be all animated by one Spirit, and be thereby united to each other and to God, through him. Thus, as the mission of Jesus was to the Jews, that of the Holy Spirit was to the church,* and that of the church to the world.†

We find, further, that the first Christian Church was that at Jerusalem; so that as the spiritual Jerusalem is the "mother" of all believers, the literal Jerusalem is the mother of all the churches of Christ on earth; and the pretensions of the Roman hierarchy, based upon the antiquity of the church afterward founded at Rome, are false and unfounded, as they are arrogant and presumptuous.

VI. The Action and Design of Baptism.

The originators of the present religious movement were, all of them, from Pedobaptist parties. They were united together as a distinct society, for the purpose of effecting Christian union, upon the principles which I have laid before you, and had been thus engaged for a considerable time before their attention was especially called to the subject of baptism. The question was at length brought up by a member, who expressed a doubt as to the lawfulness

---

* Jesus says to his disciples: "I will pray the Father and he shall give YOU another Comforter—even the Spirit of Truth, *whom the world cannot receive.*" John xiv. 17; xv. 26.

† "Ye are the salt of the earth." "Ye are the light of the world." Matt. v. "The house of God, which is the church of the living God, the pillar and support of the truth." 1 Tim. iii. 15.

of infant baptism, inasmuch as he could find neither precept nor precedent for it in the Scriptures. To this it was replied, that if the practice had not a Divine warrant, they would be obliged to relinquish it, as, according to their principles, they could regard nothing as a matter of faith or duty, for which there could not be produced clear scriptural evidence. Soon after, it was again objected, that there could be found no Divine authority for the rites of sprinkling or pouring, as modes of baptism, since the word baptism itself, as well as the language in connection with it, and all the circumstances attending the recorded baptisms of the New Testament, evidently indicated that an immersion in water was the action originally known as baptism. Upon this, the society immediately entered upon an examination of the whole subject; and, after a careful investigation, continued for a number of months, it was finally decided that there was not to be found in the Bible the slightest authority for the baptism of any one who was not a believer; and that an immersion in water was evidently the action originally indicated by the term, and practised by primitive Christians. Such conclusions, under the circumstances of the case, opposed, as they were, to the previous views and practices of those concerned, and to the popularity of the cause in which they were engaged, will weigh not a little with the candid and reflecting, as additional evidence of the force of truth, and the futility of those customs which, from tradition, convenience and carnality, have been substituted for the ordinance of Christian baptism. The views thus adopted were immediately put into practice, and have continued unchanged to this day—frequent discussion and the severest scrutiny having only tended to confirm and extend them.

It would be quite unnecessary for me to present to you here the scriptural evidences to show either that a believer is a proper subject for baptism, or that immersion is baptism. No Pedobaptist authority ever denied either of these propositions. On the contrary, they are both universally admitted to be true, and the whole controversy has been upon the questions, whether infants, who are incapable of believing, are fit subjects; and whether sprinkling, pouring, anointing, or any other action than an immersion in water, may be justly considered as a literal and true baptism? It belongs to those who take the affirmative of these questions, to prove them. This they have often attempted to do, but with what success I must leave you to judge. Suffice it to say, that the Church of Rome claims to have delivered infant baptism as a tradition to Protestants, and candid Pedobaptist Protestants admit that the practice rests wholly on church authority, and confess themselves unable to bring any direct scriptural evidence in support of it.* Of course, as we deny that mere tradition, or any assumed church authority, is a proper foundation on which to build religious institutions, we can have nothing whatever to do with the practices in question.

---

* As one among many evidences that candid Pedobaptists confess themselves unable to bring forward direct scriptural evidence in support of infant baptism, we present the following extract from the August number of the North British Review, a most able work, conducted, we believe, by Sir David Brewster, the son-in-law of Dr. Chalmers, and others. In this extract, infant baptism is acknowledged to rest on church authority alone, which was also the view of Coleridge; and although this foundation may be satisfactory to those who believe that the church has power to alter Christ's institutions, or to establish new religious rites, it leaves infant baptism without any support whatever, in the view of true Protestants, who will admit no authority in religion but the word of God:—

"The baptismal service is founded on Scripture, but its application to an unconscious infant is destitute of any express scriptural warrant. Scripture knows nothing of the baptism of infants. There is absolutely not a single trace of it to be found in the New Testament. There are passages which may be reconciled with it, if the practice can only be proved to have existed, but there is not one word which asserts its existence.

"Baptism appears in the New Testament avowedly as the rite whereby converts were incorporated into the Christian society: the burden of the proof is entirely on those who affirm its applicability to those whose minds are incapable of any conscious act of faith.

"The truth, then, is clear. The language of Scripture regarding baptism, implies the spiritual act of faith in the reci-

I wish, however, to call your attention for a moment, to the aspects of this matter, as it stands related to Christian union. Apart from the intrinsic merits of the questions which respect baptism itself, it will be seen that in adopting the action of immersion, which all grant to be valid baptism, and in admitting the believer, who is allowed by all to be a proper subject, we offer no impediment whatever to Christian union. We introduce no litigated or doubtful questions; we adopt that in which all are already agreed; we require no one to act contrary to the

pients. When infant baptism is now spoken of, the necessary modification must accordingly be made in applying language used by Scripture concerning spiritual baptism only. Inextricable confusion has been the inevitable consequence, when language used of adults, of persons possessed of intelligence, and capable of spiritual acts, was gratuitously applied to unconscious infants; and it cannot be a matter for wonder, that a totally new conception of the ordinance should have been created by such a perversion. So great was the difficulty felt to be by Luther, who retained infant baptism, and assumed that the language used of baptism in Scripture applied to the baptized infant, that in order to fence out priestly superstition, he imagined that God, who bestowed regeneration, bestowed, also, by a direct miraculous act, that intelligent faith which the spiritual nature of Christianity demanded. Our age is not likely to acquiesce in such a resolution, but it bears witness to the just perception which Luther had of the impossibility of applying to infants, without a modification somewhere, the scriptural language regarding baptism."

dictates of an enlightened conscience; we demand nothing more than what the word of God clearly and unequivocally enjoins. In this point of view, then, the position which the Reformation has assumed upon this subject, is eminently anti-sectarian and conciliatory.

Nor, if we may regard the plain declarations of Scripture as worthy of universal acceptation, or the popular creeds as fair exponents of the views of the different religious parties, are we less catholic in the sentiments which we hold in regard to the design of baptism, viz. that it is *for the remission of sins.**

To the believing penitent, we regard it as an

* It cannot be denied that Peter, on the day of Pentecost, commanded the believing penitents to be baptized for the remission of sins, nor that Ananias said to Paul, "Arise and be baptized, and wash away thy sins;" nor that the same connection between baptism and remission is asserted in many parts of Scripture. Neither can it be denied that the Episcopal Church, in its larger creed, puts into the mouth of the believer these words: "I acknowledge one baptism for the remission of sins;" nor that in its 27th Article (on baptism) it says:

"Baptism is not only a sign of profession and mark of difference, whereby Christian men are discerned from others that are not christened; but it is also a sign of regeneration or new birth, whereby, as by an instrument, they that receive baptism rightly, are grafted into the church, and the promises of the forgiveness of sins, and of our adoption to be the sons of God by the Holy Spirit, are *visibly signed and sealed.*"

Neither can it be denied, that in the practical application of *assurance* of actual forgiveness, or, as clearly expressed in the Westminster Confession, "a *sign* and *seal* of remission of sins." It is, then, to the believer, the *sign*, *evidence*, or *assurance* of pardon, and

---

these views the minister is instructed to say to those presenting themselves for baptism:

"Beloved, ye hear, in this gospel, the express words of our Saviour Christ, that, except a man be born of water and of the Spirit, he cannot enter into the kingdom of God. Whereby ye may perceive the great necessity of this sacrament, where it may be had. Likewise, immediately before his ascension into heaven, (as we read in the last chapter of Saint Mark,) he gave command to his disciples, saying, Go ye into all the world and preach the gospel to every creature. He that believeth and is baptized shall be saved; but he that believeth not shall be damned; which also showeth unto us the great benefit we reap thereby. For which cause, St. Peter, the apostle, when upon his first preaching of the gospel, many were pricked at the heart, and said to him and the rest of the apostles, Men and brethren what shall we do? replied and said unto them, Repent and be baptized every one of you for the remission of sins, and ye shall receive the gift of the Holy Ghost; for the promise is to you and to your children, and to all that are afar off, even as many as the Lord our God shall call. And with many other words exhorted he them, saying, Save yourselves from this untoward generation. For, as the same apostle testifieth in another place, even baptism doth now save us, (not the putting away of the filth of the flesh, but the answer of a good conscience toward God,) by the resurrection of Jesus Christ. Doubt ye not, therefore, but earnestly believe that he will favorably receive these present persons, truly repenting, and coming unto him by faith, that he will grant them remission

not the *procuring cause* of pardon. This is a distinction which it is important to make, since the very same language is used in reference to the design of Christ's sacrifice. He says himself, "this is

---

of their sins, and bestow upon them the Holy Ghost; that he will give them the blessing of eternal life, and make them partakers of his everlasting kingdom."

Nor is it to be denied, that the Westminster Confession of Faith expresses itself to the same effect, as follows:

"Baptism is a sacrament of the New Testament, ordained by Jesus Christ, not only for the solemn admission of the party baptized into the visible church; but also to be unto him a *sign* and *seal* of the covenant of grace, of his engrafting into Christ, of regeneration, *of remission of sins*, and of his giving up unto God, through Jesus Christ, to walk in newness of life; which sacrament is, by Christ's own appointment, to be continued in his church until the end of the world."

Nor, finally, can it be controverted, that while the Methodist Discipline adopts, in substance, the Episcopal form, the Baptist creed says:

"Baptism is an ordinance of the New Testament, ordained by Jesus Christ, to be unto the party baptized a sign of his fellowship with him in his death and resurrection; of his being engrafted into him; *of remission of sins*, and of his giving up unto God, through Jesus Christ, to live and walk in newness of life."

But I need not multiply quotations from the Scriptures, to show that baptism is for the remission of sins, or that it is in this ordinance that an individual is born of water, according to the declaration of Christ in John iii. 5. Neither is it necessary for me to make further extracts from the creeds to show that they do most unequivocally acknowledge the same truths.

my blood, shed *for the remission of sins.*" Nay, we find that salvation or pardon is, in the Scriptures, attributed to various other causes, as faith, grace, obedience, repentance, &c. But who does not see, that while salvation may be thus attributed to any one or all of these, it cannot be supposed to be connected with them all in the same sense? In fact, is it not obvious, that while, as all admit, the blood or sacrifice of Christ is the *procuring* cause of our salvation, it is through faith, repentance, and baptism that the sinner finds access to that sacrifice, and that he may hence be said to believe unto salvation, or to be baptized for the remission of sins, as the means of attaining to the *actual and personal enjoyment* of the salvation purchased by the death of Christ? All these means of enjoyment are necessary, but each in its proper place and order, and, among them, baptism is especially distinguished as the *remitting ordinance,* or formal pledge of pardon —a position which, from its symbolic and emblematic character, it is so eminently fitted to occupy. Thus it is called the "washing of regeneration," through which we are introduced into the kingdom of God, and we are said to be "buried with Christ by baptism into death," to be "baptized into Christ's death," &c. The simple fact that we *put on Christ* in baptism, is abundantly sufficient to show that we must find in it a pledge of pardon; for he who puts on or receives Christ must also receive his salvation. No one can be in Christ and in his sins at the same time. "If any man be in Christ, he is a new creature: old things are passed away; behold, all things are become new." It is in immersion, accordingly, that the penitent *believer* puts off "the body of the sins of the flesh" and becomes a partaker of the benefits of the death of Christ, and it is in it also that he is raised again with him "to walk in newness of life."

It must be acknowledged, however, that while we thus most cordially assent to what both the Scriptures and the creeds expressly say, that baptism is for the remission of sins, the sects at present existing (if we except, perhaps, the Episcopal) do by no means assent to it, and, upon this subject, believe neither the Scriptures nor their own creeds. This seems to be owing chiefly to the fact, that a particular theory of spiritual operations, which has gradually almost entirely monopolized the minds of the Protestant community, makes the assurance of pardon to rest on certain feelings, or upon what are thought to be supernatural visions, or special spiritual communications. The attempt is thus made to transfer the office of baptism, as the remitting ordinance, to vague, emotional, or mental impressions; and to effect this purpose, the connection of baptism with the remission of sins is totally denied; nor is there a single individual in any of these parties, who is taught to regard baptism *practically*, as a pledge or assurance of pardon.

It is greatly to be deplored, that a mere theory of conversion should have so engrossed the attention of the religious world, and that it should have exercised so deleterious an influence upon the minds of the unconverted, as to lead them to neglect and disparage positive Divine institutions, and the appointed means through which the assurance of pardon is actually bestowed. Nevertheless, we would not, by any means, desire to underrate the importance of the work of the Holy Spirit, or of a change of heart. No one can be born again, unless he is born of Spirit as well as of water, and no one can enjoy the remission of sins who is not thus regenerated; but we cannot consent that the peculiar object or purpose assigned to baptism in the Scriptures should be *transferred* to any internal operations or feelings, without Divine authority. In the present instance, the Scriptures do, in various forms of speech, assert the connection between baptism and remission, but they nowhere teach that any mental impressions, visions, or extraordinary visitations, are to be regarded as evidences of pardon; nor is it anywhere said, that men are *to receive the Holy Spirit for the remission of sins.* This brings me, however, to the consideration of spiritual influence, which is next in order.

VII. The Agency of the Holy Spirit in Conversion and Sanctification.

The chief cause of misapprehension in regard to spiritual influence, is, as it appears to me, to be found in the fact, that most persons confound the agency of the Spirit in the *conversion of the sinner*, with the influence he exerts as *indwelling in the heart of the believer*. Hence the vague and unscriptural notion, that the Spirit may be received before faith, and that faith itself is something wrought in the heart by a special and supernatural operation of the Spirit. This, indeed, seems to be, with many, the beginning and the end of all spiritual influence, and they depend, accordingly, upon certain mental or emotional impressions, of which they have once been the subjects, for their evidence of conversion, their assurance of pardon, their means of sanctification, and their hope of heaven.

We regard, however, the conversion of the sinner and the sanctification of the believer, as distinct matters, accomplished, indeed, by the same Spirit, but in a different manner, and from a widely different position. We conceive the Holy Spirit to stand to the sinner in a relation very distinct from that in which he stands to him who is a member of the family of God. With the former, he is an outward witness for the truth; but the latter "has the witness *in himself.*" To the first he is an unknown visitant or stranger; to the last, he is an indwelling and cherished guide. To the sinner, he is as the rain which falls upon the surface of the earth to soften and subdue: to the believer, he is as a fountain *from within,* springing up unto everlasting life. In short, to bring the matter at once to issue, we deny that there is any scriptural authority for the notion that the unbeliever, or man of the world, can *receive* the Spirit of God. We hold this dogma to be in direct opposition to the Divine testimony, since Christ himself declares to his disciples that he would pray the Father, and He would give to them another Comforter, "even the Spirit of Truth," continues he, "WHOM THE WORLD CANNOT RECEIVE." (John xiv. 17.)

That which is pure, must be received into a pure vessel; and it is not until the heart is "purified by faith," that the Holy Spirit may enter to dwell therein. This is the view everywhere given in the Scriptures. Peter said to the believing penitents on the day of Pentecost, "Reform and be baptized for the remission of sins, and you shall [then] receive the gift of the Holy Spirit." Paul wrote to the Ephesians, "in Christ ye also trusted, after that ye heard the word of truth, the gospel of your salvation, in whom, also, *after that ye believed,* ye were sealed with that Holy Spirit of promise, which is the earnest of our inheritance." And also to the Galatians: "*Because ye are sons,* God hath sent forth the Spirit of his Son into your hearts, crying Abba, Father." It is, on the other hand, nowhere stated that the Holy Spirit was *given* to any one to make him a believer, or a child of God.

But you may ask, is not every convert born of the Spirit? Must not every one be regenerated before entering the kingdom of heaven? True, but being "*born* of the Spirit," or *regenerated,* and *receiving* the Spirit, are matters quite different. No one can be born by *receiving* the Spirit. No one can be born of any thing that he *receives,* for the simple reason that he must be first born before he can receive any thing. Hence the Scriptures say that the Spirit is *given* to those who "are sons." How, then, you will inquire, is an individual "born of the Spirit?" In order to comprehend this, we must be careful to maintain consistency in our interpretation of the figure, and must remember that, in the Scriptures, comparisons are employed with the utmost suitableness and accuracy, in illustration of the particular points to which they are applied.

The figure of a *spiritual* birth is drawn from a natural or *literal* birth; a *re*-generation from a *generation.* Hence, in all leading points, a just resemblance must be preserved between the fact and the figure. This we find, accordingly, in the language which the Scripture uses wherever this striking figure is introduced. James says, "God, according to his own will, hath *begotten* us by the word of truth." Peter says, we are "regenerated, not of corruptible *seed*, but incorruptible, even of the word of God, which lives and abides for ever." Paul says to the Corinthians: "Though ye have ten thousand instructors in Christ, yet have ye not many fathers, for in Christ Jesus I have begotten you *through the gospel*." And John says: "Whosoever believeth *that Jesus is the Christ*, is begotten [born] of God." It is the gospel, then, which constitutes the incorruptible seed of which the children of God are born; as in the parallel figure of the sower, (Matt. xiii.,) it is the gospel of the kingdom which is sown by the Son of man, and which, falling into good and honest hearts, brings forth abundant fruit to God. To believe that great proposition, that *Jesus is the Christ*, is, in John's expressive language, to be "begotten of God." It is thus with this sublime proposition and its proofs, as we formerly stated, that *God first meets the sinner*. In a word, it is the *gospel* that is *received* by the sinner, and not the Holy Spirit. Yet if he receive that gospel, spoken by the apostles in words inspired by the Holy Spirit, preached by them "with the Holy Spirit sent down from heaven," and "confirmed by demonstrations of the Spirit and of power," he is justly said to be "begotten of God," or of the Spirit, "through the word of truth;" and when, at his baptism, he comes forth from the water as from the womb, the figure of regeneration is complete; he is born of water and Spirit;* he is born again "from above." Being thus born from above, he is prepared to *receive* that Spirit of adoption, that Holy Spirit or Comforter, which God bestows upon all his children, and which becomes to them an internal indwelling witness, and an earnest of their eternal inheritance, and produces in them, through its sanctifying influences and those of the truth it has revealed, the precious fruits of love, joy, peace, and righteousness.

The communication of the Holy Spirit may, then, be justly regarded as the great end of the ministration of the gospel. Unless the Holy Spirit be received and enjoyed, all faith, all forms, all professions

---

* Persons sometimes wonder why these words should be placed in this order, and why the water should not be mentioned last, since immersion follows, in order of time, the spiritual influence of the gospel. A moment's reflection, however, will show that this is the proper order, and the one actually most appropriate from the nature of the figure. A child, literally, *must be born of its mother, before it can be said to be born of its father,* and such is precisely the order of enunciation observed in the figure.

are alike nugatory and vain. "If any man have not the Spirit of Christ, he is none of his," and consequently can have no heirship with him; no sonship to God; no earnest of a future inheritance. The possession of the Spirit is indeed the very evidence of sonship, and the proof that the gospel has been truly believed.

Nor is this enjoyment of the Holy Spirit momentary or transient in its nature, as many seem to think who mistake for it those evanescent excitements of feeling which may attend conversion. The Comforter is to abide with the Christian for ever, and the latter is hence taught to seek "the supply of the Spirit of Christ;" to ask, that he may receive; to seek, that he may find; to knock, that it may be opened to him. "For if you, being evil," said Christ to the disciples, "know how to give good gifts to your children, how much more shall your heavenly Father give the Holy Spirit to them that ask him." The graces and the blessedness of the Christian are alike "fruits of the Spirit." The peace of God which passeth all understanding, and which keeps his heart and mind; the joy that animates, and the love which warms his soul, are inward feelings or emotions which must be produced by the presence of the Divine Spirit, no less than those outward works of piety and humanity which the gospel enjoins. The true kingdom of God, in short, is within the heart, and consists in "righteousness, peace, and joy in the Holy Spirit."

This, I presume, is a sufficient explanation of our views upon the subject legitimately before us. That there are various obstacles and hindrances which often prevent the gospel from reaching the heart of the sinner; and that there are, on the other hand, various agencies, ministerial and providential, human and Divine, general and special, which tend to remove these obstacles, and thus enable the gospel to exert its power, we freely admit. And hence it is necessary to seek these agencies, and proper to expect that God will, in answer to prayer, cause his word to be glorified in the conversion of those in whose behalf it is our duty and our privilege to ask his gracious interposition.

Nor do we deem it at all necessary that any controversy should exist with regard to the *nature* or mode of action of those influences which promote conversion. Certain it is that the same result will be effected, if these influences merely remove the impediments of ignorance, inattention, and love of the world, or any others which may obstruct the action of the gospel, as if they were to give such increased power and efficiency to the gospel itself, as to enable it to break through and overcome these obstacles. If, as Paul intimates, (2 Cor. iv. 3, 4,) "the god of this world blinds by its perishing things the minds of those who believe not, lest the light of the glorious gospel of Christ should shine unto them,"* certainly those agencies which would simply remove the obstructions he interposes, would enable the light of the gospel to reach the heart of the sinner just as effectually as would an increase of light sufficient to *penetrate* these obstructions. It is not necessary that the light of the sun be increased a thousandfold in order that it may pierce the clouds that intercept it: all that is needed is, that these clouds be removed, when his beams will at once illuminate and warm whatever is thus exposed to them.

To say that the gospel requires a *positive* addition of power to enable it to reach the heart, is to say that it is *really* deficient in power. But does not its power consist in the love of God which it reveals? How, then, could its power be augmented, unless by the addition of new facts, and nobler or more attractive views of God? But the gospel can receive no such addition, and consequently no increase of power. It is already "the power of God," and they who imagine it to have received additional power in their own experience, are unable to mention a single new fact or idea from which such additional power could be derived. But, as said before, it is quite unnecessary that any controversy should exist on the

* Macknight's version.

subject of converting influence. All should be content to preach the gospel and prayerfully commit the event to God, confident that though even a Paul may plant and an Apollos water, it is He alone that giveth the increase. As well might hnsbandmen neglect to sow their fields in order to debate with each other their respective theories in regard to the mode in which the seed is made to vegetate, as laborers of the Divine "husbandry," instead of preaching the gospel, occupy themselves with unprofitable discussions as to the *mode* in which God is pleased to render his word effective to salvation. We deprecate, therefore, the adoption of any theory upon this subject, and desire only to urge the claims of the gospel, as, at least, the only revealed instrumentality through which the Spirit of God accomplishes the conversion of the sinner. What influences he may exert in aid of the gospel, and in what particular *manner* the heart is "*opened*" for its reception, we regard as questions entirely subordinate, and as matters of opinion about which men may differ, without any just cause or occasion of disunion.

We deem it unfortunate, however, that any sentiments should gain currency in reference to this matter, which either, on the one hand, tend to depreciate and render ineffectual the word of God; or, on the other, to represent God as a mere inactive spectator of the progress of the gospel. The Spirit of God is not to be separated from the word; neither is the word to be separated from the Spirit, in the great work of man's salvation. The former view opens the door to wild enthusiasm and every species of delusion; while the latter leads to a cold, abstract, undevotional philosophy, under whose influence true *heartfelt* religion declines and perishes. That men are "regenerated by the incorruptible seed of the word," and sanctified "through the truth," the Scripture distinctly affirms; as it does, also, that it is "the Spirit that quickeneth," and that Christians are God's "workmanship, created in Christ Jesus unto good works." It should be sufficient for all reverently to believe these revealed truths, without presuming to theorize and dogmatize in regard to the particular *mode* in which either the word or the Spirit accomplishes the Divine purpose.

VIII. Weekly Communion.

As we read in the Scriptures, that "on the first-day of the week the disciples came together to break bread;" and as the records show that it was the invariable custom of the early Christians to commemorate the death of Christ on every first-day of the week, we conceive that this order should be carefully maintained and attended to by all the churches now. We regard it as the great and special object of the Lord's-day meeting thus to commemorate the love of Christ, but it is usual to add prayer, exhortation, teaching, &c., for mutual edification. Since pious and learned men of various parties have often deplored the departure of the modern churches from this ancient order of things, and have labored to restore the weekly observance of the Lord's Supper, we may justly regard the practice as sanctioned by the best authority, and its propriety placed beyond the reach of controversy.

From among those who have borne testimony upon this subject, I would adduce *John Brown*, of Haddington, who wrote a treatise upon it, in which he strongly advocated weekly communion. William King, also, Archbishop of Dublin, speaks as follows: "It is manifest that if it be not our own faults, we may have opportunity every Lord's day when we meet together, and, therefore, that church is guilty of laying aside the command, whose order and worship doth not require and provide for this practice." Dr. Scott, in his commentary on Acts xx. 7, says: "*Breaking of bread*, or commemorating the death of Christ in the Eucharist, was one chief end of their assembling: this ordinance seems to have been *constantly administered every Lord's day.*" Dr. Mason, of New York, asserts that, "Communion every Lord's day was universal, and was preserved in the Greek church till the seventh century."* Calvin complains of the neglect of this practice: "It ought to have been," says he, "far otherwise. *Every week*, at least, the table of the Lord should have been spread for Christian assemblies, and the promises declared, by which, partaking of it, we might be spiritually fed."† John Wesley urged the same practice. In his letter to America, he says: "I also advise the elders to administer the supper of the Lord *on every Lord's day*."

Such, then, is the universal usage with us. We recognise, also, the importance of Sunday-schools and Bible classes for the instruction of the young; and of wholly consecrating the Lord's day to the above purposes, as well as to private reading of the Scriptures and religious devotion.

IX. Church Government.

The Lord Jesus Christ, the great Shepherd of the flock, has committed the care of his church to pastors, or under-shepherds, who are commanded to "feed the flock of God," taking the oversight thereof, not by constraint, but willingly; not for filthy lucre,

* Dr. John Mason's Letters on Frequent Communion.

† Inst. lib. vi. chap. xviii. sect. 56.

but of a ready mind. In the Scriptures, pastors are sometimes called bishops, or overseers, from the nature of their duty, and sometimes elders, from the fact that they are usually possessed of age and experience. Their qualifications and duties are clearly stated in the letters to Timothy and Titus; in Paul's address to the elders of the church at Ephesus, &c. They have charge of the spiritual interests of the church, and are to be supported in their labors according to the circumstances of the case, and their devotion, ability, usefulness, &c. There should be a plurality of them in every church, as was evidently the case in primitive times. Paul addresses the church at Philippi, "*with the bishops and deacons.*" Paul sent for the *elders of the church* at Ephesus, who seem, from his address to them, to have been a numerous body. Paul left Titus in Crete, to *ordain elders in every city.* There is no such thing recognised in Scripture as a bishop over a diocese, containing a plurality of churches; and as to the arrogant pretensions of popes and prelates, who claim to come in place of the apostles, and to sit in the temple of God as representatives of Divinity, we find them only in the prophetic account which the apostles have given of the rise and development of the Man of Sin. In the very nature of things, the apostles could have no successors. They were appointed by Christ *in person,* as his *witnesses*, and it was absolutely essential to their office that they should have *seen* the Lord, and have had a *personal knowledge of his resurrection from the dead.* It was requisite, also, that they should have the power of working miracles, and other supernatural gifts, as *proofs* of their mission as Christ's ambassadors to the world. The gospel being fully delivered, and the testimony completed, this office could no longer continue. We recognise, accordingly, as rulers in the church, only the *elders* or *overseers* of each congregation, whose authority is restricted to the particular church by which they are chosen.

We have another class of officers, called *deacons*, whose duty it is to take charge of the temporal affairs of the church and minister to the sick, the poor, and the destitute. *Evangelists* or *missionaries* are also sustained by the churches, in the work of preaching the gospel to the world.

I present to you, then, my dear friend, the preceding brief account of the chief matters urged upon the religious community in the present reformation movement. That Christian union can be effected by a return to the original principles of the gospel, and in no other way, is, I hope, by this time, sufficiently evident. Simple principles, and not elaborate systems and doubtful opinions, must form the rallying point. The fundamental principles of Protestantism, and the common Christianity of the religious world furnish, indeed, a present basis for the co-operation of all; and nothing is needed, with the Divine blessing, but the proper application of these principles, and the disentanglement of this common Christianity from the perplexed maze in which it is involved.

And oh! how desirable is a real Christian union in view of the present circumstances and future prospects of the church and the world. In the present rapid movements of society; in the spread of civilization; the increasing intercourse and fraternization of mankind; the opening of every region of the earth to missionary enterprise, and the manifest approach of the great day in which the Lord shall come to be "glorified in his saints," and to take vengeance on those "who know not God and obey not the gospel," how important that believers should present an unbroken front, and maintain that unity, without which, the conversion of the world and the perfection of the church, would seem to be alike impossible!

R. R.

THE END.

www.ingramcontent.com/pod-product-compliance
Lightning Source LLC
LaVergne TN
LVHW011120110826
845150LV00008B/2202

* 9 7 8 1 4 2 5 5 0 4 5 6 4 *